NOAH LYLES: Fastest Kid on the Track

James R. Delacruz

Noah Lyles

Noah Lyles

TABLE OF CONTENTS

Noah Lyles

INTRODUCTION

Noah Lyles wasn't always the world-famous sprinter we know today. He was once a young kid just like you, filled with dreams and big goals! Growing up, Noah faced plenty of challenges, but he never let anything hold him back. With a lot of hard work, determination, and support from his family, he turned his dreams into reality.

In Noah Lyles: Fastest Kid on the Track, you'll learn how Noah's love for running began and how he worked hard to become one of the fastest people on the planet. From overcoming setbacks to setting new records, Noah's journey is filled with inspiring lessons and exciting moments. Whether you're a track fan or simply love stories of people following their dreams, Noah's story will motivate you to reach for your own goals.

Let's dive in and discover the incredible journey of Noah Lyles—an athlete who shows us that with courage and perseverance, anything is possible!

CHAPTER 1: WHO IS NOAH LYLES

Noah Lyles is an American sprinter and one of the fastest runners in the world. Known for his explosive speed and energetic personality, he specializes in the 100-meter and 200-meter sprints. Born in 1997 in Gainesville, Florida, Noah showed a love for running from a young age, competing in youth track events with his brother, Josephus.

Throughout his career, Noah has won multiple gold medals in international competitions, including the World Championships, and set several records in sprinting. In 2019, he ran the 200 meters in 19.50 seconds, making him one of the fastest ever in that event. Noah is also known for his unique style and for celebrating his victories in fun ways, like dancing or striking memorable poses after races.

Beyond his achievements on the track, Noah is passionate about inspiring young athletes and is open about overcoming challenges, including struggles with his mental health. His story shows that with determination, positivity, and hard work, incredible goals can be achieved.

Noah Lyles

THE EARLY DAYS

Noah Lyles' journey started long before he became a household name in track and field. Born on July 18, 1997, in Gainesville, Florida, Noah grew up in a family that loved sports. His parents, Keisha and Kevin Lyles were both athletes who encouraged him and his brother, Josephus, to be active and work hard toward their dreams. From a young age, Noah was full of energy, running around the playground faster than the other kids. His family noticed his talent, but they also saw his joy in running and how much he loved competing.

As Noah got older, he joined youth track teams and began training seriously. Alongside his brother, he started winning races and catching the attention of coaches. The Lyles brothers became known for their incredible speed and teamwork, pushing each other to improve and celebrate each other's victories. Even though there were challenges along the way, Noah's early experiences in track and field gave him the foundation he needed to succeed later on.

Those early days weren't just about winning races—they were about discovering his passion and learning that, with hard work, anything was possible.

Noah Lyles

DISCOVERING A LOVE FOR RUNNING

Noah Lyles' love for running began with the simplest moments—dashing around the playground and racing his friends in his neighborhood. Even as a young kid, he had an energy that seemed endless, always wanting to go faster and beat his times. His speed and excitement didn't go unnoticed, especially by his family. His parents, both former athletes, quickly realized Noah had a natural talent for running.

When he joined his first track team, Noah felt right at home. He loved the feeling of sprinting across the track, the wind rushing past him as he pushed his limits. Unlike many kids his age, he didn't shy away from the hard work and effort needed to improve. Each practice was a chance to learn, and each race was an opportunity to do his best. Running wasn't just a sport to Noah—it was something he looked forward to every day, a way to challenge himself and a place where he felt he truly belonged.

GROWING UP WITH BIG DREAMS

From the start, Noah Lyles had dreams that went beyond just winning races. Even as a young kid, he imagined himself standing on big stages, competing in world-famous events like the Olympics. Inspired by legendary sprinters he watched on TV, he dreamed of one day being just like them—maybe even faster.

With each passing year, his dreams grew bigger, and so did his determination. His family and coaches encouraged him, reminding him that hard work and dedication could make those dreams come true. Noah took that advice to heart. He trained hard, studied other runners, and set goals for himself. If he lost a race, he didn't give up; he just pushed himself to do better next time. Every time he hit the track, he was one step closer to his dream.

Noah's big dreams kept him focused, even when things got tough. He knew that reaching for something great wouldn't be easy, but he was ready to face whatever challenges came his way. Growing up with those big dreams gave him the courage and motivation he needed to chase his goals, no matter how far they seemed.

As Noah grew older, his dreams continued to shape him. In middle school and high school, he became known as "the fast kid"—the one who everyone knew would go places. But his dreams were never just about winning medals or setting records; they were about proving to himself that he could accomplish anything he set his mind to. Noah wanted to inspire others, too, showing kids like him that big dreams weren't just for grown-ups.

In high school, Noah started competing in more serious track events, and the path to his dreams began to come into focus. He faced new challenges, like harder training and tougher competition, but he welcomed them. Noah knew that every tough workout, every loss, and every victory was helping him get closer to his goal. Alongside his brother, Josephus, who shared his passion, he learned how important teamwork and family support were to keep going strong.

He also began visualizing his dreams—picturing himself crossing the finish line at the Olympics, hearing the crowd roar, and representing his country on the world stage. These dreams kept him grounded and motivated, helping him stay focused on his journey. With each race, Noah saw his dreams come closer to becoming a reality, knowing that every step he took was one step closer to fulfilling the dreams he had as a kid.

CHAPTER 2: CHALLENGES ON THE TRACK

Noah Lyles' journey to becoming one of the fastest sprinters in the world wasn't always smooth. Along the way, he faced numerous challenges that tested his dedication and resilience. One of the biggest hurdles came in the form of injuries. Like many athletes, Noah experienced setbacks in training and races due to strains and muscle issues. Each time he was injured, he had to take a break from running—a frustrating pause for someone so determined to succeed. But instead of giving up, Noah used these moments to grow stronger. He focused on recovery, listened to his coaches, and worked on areas that would make him more resilient in the future.

Noah also faced the mental challenge of dealing with pressure. As he gained more attention in the world of track and field, expectations grew. He knew people were watching, hoping to see him break records and bring home medals. Balancing his passion for the sport with this pressure was tough at times. He had to learn to tune out the noise and focus on what mattered most: his love for running and his personal goals.

There were also races where things simply didn't go as planned. Losing a race, especially after months of hard work, was difficult. But Noah learned to see these moments as valuable lessons. Instead of getting discouraged, he analyzed his mistakes and used them to improve his technique, speed, and mental toughness. Overcoming these challenges taught him that failure is just another step on the path to success.

Through every challenge, Noah grew stronger and more determined. He learned that true champions aren't just the ones who win every
 race—they're the ones who keep going, even when the road gets tough.

FACING SETBACKS AND INJURIES

Even the fastest runners in the world face setbacks, and Noah Lyles is no exception. As he worked hard to improve and push his limits, injuries became part of his journey. Whether it was a pulled muscle, a sprained ankle, or a more serious strain, Noah had to learn how to deal with these painful obstacles. Each injury meant stepping away from training and races, which was tough for someone who loved running so much.

But Noah didn't let these setbacks stop him. Instead of feeling discouraged, he focused on getting better. He worked closely with his doctors and trainers to heal properly, and during his recovery, he kept his mind focused on his long-term goals. He reminded himself that taking time to heal would make him stronger and faster when he returned to the track.

During these breaks, Noah also spent time studying his own races, watching video footage, and working on strengthening different parts of his body that might help prevent future injuries. He realized that setbacks weren't the end of the road—they were an important part of learning how to be a better athlete.

Facing injuries and setbacks taught Noah how to be patient and persistent. He learned that sometimes the best thing you can do after a challenge is to rest, recover, and come back even stronger than before.

LEARNING FROM LOSSES

Noah Lyles didn't always win every race. Some of his biggest lessons came from the losses he experienced. Losing can be tough, especially when you've trained hard and given it your all. But Noah quickly realized that losing wasn't the end of the world—it was just an opportunity to learn and grow.

Noah Lyles

After a loss, instead of being discouraged, Noah took time to analyze what went wrong. Did he start the race too slowly? Was there something in his form that he could improve? He didn't shy away from looking at his mistakes; instead, he used them to motivate himself to work harder. Each loss taught him something new—whether it was a better way to train or a mental lesson about how to stay focused under pressure.

Noah's losses also helped him build resilience. He understood that even the greatest athletes face tough moments. The key is not to let one loss define you but to keep pushing forward. He learned that setbacks and defeats were part of the journey, and the most important thing was to get back up, keep training, and never stop chasing his dreams.

By learning from his losses, Noah became not only a faster runner but also a smarter one. He knew that each race, whether a win or a loss, was a chance to improve and become better than before.

Noah also realized that losses helped him grow mentally. It was easy to feel frustrated or upset after a defeat, but he learned how important it was to stay positive. Instead of focusing on the disappointment, he began to view losses as a chance to develop a stronger mindset. He understood that confidence wasn't just built on wins; it was built on how you handle adversity.

In those moments of defeat, Noah reminded himself why he loved running in the first place: the thrill of competition, the desire to improve, and the excitement of setting new personal goals. Losing a race didn't mean he wasn't talented—it just meant he had something new to work on. This mindset helped him keep going, even when the road got tough.

Noah's ability to bounce back after losses also inspired others. Many young athletes look up to him and see how he handles challenges with grace and determination. His story shows that losses don't define who you are as an athlete or a person; it's how you respond to them that counts.

In the end, Noah's losses taught him valuable lessons about perseverance, humility, and the power of learning from mistakes. With every race, win or lose, he grew stronger and more prepared for the next challenge. And that made his victories even sweeter when they came.

CHAPTER 3: TRAINING FOR GREATNESS

Becoming one of the fastest sprinters in the world didn't happen overnight. For Noah Lyles, it took years of hard work, sweat, and a commitment to being the best he could be. His training wasn't just about running as fast as possible; it was about building strength, improving his technique, and pushing himself to do things that most people thought were impossible.

Noah's training schedule was intense. Every day, he focused on different aspects of sprinting: speed, endurance, strength, and recovery. His workouts included long sprints, short bursts of high-speed running, weight training to build muscle, and exercises to improve his agility and flexibility. He didn't just run; he worked on the little details that made him faster—things like his start off the blocks, his stride, and how to keep his body relaxed while running at full speed.

But training wasn't only about physical strength. Noah also worked hard on his mental game. Being mentally tough is just as important as being physically strong when it comes to sprinting. He practiced staying focused and positive, no matter how tough the race or the workout. He learned how to push through moments of doubt and keep going when it felt like he couldn't.

Along with his coaches, Noah also spent time studying other sprinters, learning from their techniques, and figuring out what worked best for him. He was always trying to improve and find new ways to train smarter. Noah knew that to achieve greatness, he had to be willing to put in the time, energy, and effort every single day, even when it felt hard.

His dedication paid off in the form of faster times and stronger performances. But more than just running fast, Noah's training for greatness taught him about discipline, perseverance, and the importance of always striving to be better.

DAILY LIFE OF A YOUNG ATHLETE

For Noah Lyles, being a young athlete meant balancing his passion for running with his daily responsibilities. His life was full of early mornings, hard work, and focus on training, but also moments of fun and relaxation to recharge.

Noah Lyles

A typical day for Noah started early. Most mornings, he woke up before the sun, getting a good breakfast to fuel his body for the busy day ahead. His meals were carefully planned to give him the energy he needed for intense workouts, focusing on proteins, fruits, and vegetables. After eating, it was time to get ready for training.

Training usually began with a warm-up session, where Noah would stretch and do light exercises to prepare his muscles. Then it was time for the main workout, which could range from sprint drills to strength training. During sprint drills, he focused on perfecting his form and building speed. He also spent time doing weightlifting exercises to increase his strength, as building muscle helps runners explode out of the starting blocks and maintain speed during the race. After a tough workout, recovery was just as important. Noah would stretch, rest, and sometimes do light exercises to keep his muscles from getting too sore.

When he wasn't training, Noah focused on schoolwork, hanging out with friends, and enjoying time with his family. Balancing academics and athletics wasn't always easy, but Noah knew that both were important. His parents made sure he stayed on top of his homework and school projects, even if it meant spending extra time in the evening to finish assignments.

Despite his busy schedule, Noah always found time to relax and have fun. Whether it was playing video games, listening to music, or just chilling with his brother, he understood the importance of staying balanced. This allowed him to recharge and be ready to train again the next day.

Noah's daily life as a young athlete wasn't easy, but it taught him discipline, responsibility, and the importance of working hard to achieve his dreams. It also showed him how to balance work and play—an important lesson for any young athlete.

STRENGTH AND SPEED WORKOUTS

To become one of the fastest sprinters in the world, Noah Lyles had to build both strength and speed. His workouts were designed to make him faster, stronger, and more powerful on the track. These strength and speed workouts were a big part of his training and helped him improve with every race.

Speed Workouts

Noah Lyles

Speed training focused on improving how quickly Noah could run during a race. He did exercises like short sprints, where he would run at full speed for 30 to 60 meters, trying to push his limits each time. These short bursts of intense running helped him improve his acceleration and the power he needed at the beginning of a race. He also worked on his form, practicing things like staying low in the starting blocks and using his arms to help drive his body forward.

Another important part of Noah's speed workouts was "flying sprints." These were a type of sprint where Noah would gradually increase his speed over a longer distance, then race at full speed for 20 to 30 meters. These helped improve his top speed and teach his body how to maintain fast running form over a longer distance.

Strength Workouts

Building strength was just as important as building speed. To be fast, a runner needs strong muscles that can propel them forward with each step. Noah worked on strength training to build his legs, core, and upper body. His workout included exercises like squats and lunges to strengthen his legs, as well as exercises like planks and leg raises to work his core. These exercises made him more powerful and helped him run with better technique.

Noah Lyles

Noah also did exercises to build upper body strength, including push-ups, pull-ups, and weightlifting. A strong upper body helped him maintain proper form and helped his arms move efficiently as he ran. His coach focused on full-body strength because sprinters need to use every muscle in their body when running fast.

By combining strength and speed workouts, Noah trained his body to be a powerful and efficient runner. These workouts made him faster off the starting line, helped him run stronger during the race, and gave him the endurance he needed to keep going at top speed. They also taught him that being a great sprinter requires more than just running—it's about building strength, perfecting form, and staying focused every step of the way.

CHAPTER 4: RISING TO THE TOP

Noah Lyles' journey to becoming one of the fastest sprinters in the world wasn't just about hard work—it was about perseverance, believing in himself, and taking every opportunity to showcase his talent. As he continued to train and race, he quickly moved up the ranks in track and field. He started winning local races, and soon, he was competing at national events, where his incredible speed caught the attention of coaches and scouts.

Noah's rise to the top wasn't without its challenges. As he faced tougher competition, he had to continually push himself to improve. But instead of feeling overwhelmed, Noah used every race as a chance to learn and grow. His determination and hard work began to pay off in bigger ways, and soon he was breaking records and winning medals.

In 2016, at just 19 years old, Noah made his mark on the world stage by winning a gold medal in the 200 meters at the World Junior Championships. This was just the beginning of his rise to the top. By 2019, Noah was setting world-class times and becoming a favorite in international competitions. His 200-meter race at the World Championships in 2019, where he ran 19.50 seconds, made him one of the fastest sprinters in history.

Noah's incredible performances earned him spots in prestigious events like the World Championships and the Olympics. With each win, his confidence grew, and he began to see his dream of becoming an Olympic champion closer than ever before. But even as his fame grew, Noah never lost sight of what mattered: doing his best and inspiring others to chase their dreams.

Through hard work, overcoming obstacles, and never giving up, Noah rose to the top of his sport, becoming a role model for young athletes everywhere. His journey teaches us that with dedication
With, a positive attitude, and a belief in your abilities, you can achieve incredible things.

BREAKING RECORDS AND WINNING RACES

As Noah Lyles continued to train and race, his hard work paid off in a big way. He didn't just win races—he broke records and became one of the best sprinters in the world. With every competition, Noah pushed himself harder, and his incredible speed helped him achieve remarkable results.

One of Noah's most memorable achievements came in 2019 when he ran the 200 meters in 19.50 seconds at the World Championships in Doha. This performance not only earned him the gold medal but also made him one of the fastest sprinters in history. His time was just shy of the world record, but it was still a huge milestone for Noah and track and field. People began to recognize Noah as a true champion, capable of achieving even greater things.

His ability to consistently break personal and competition records earned him more victories on the world stage. He won gold at the 2019 World Championships in both the 200-meter and the 4x100-meter relay, proving that he could dominate in both individual and team events. Noah's performances in these races showed that he wasn't just fast—he was becoming a force to be reckoned with.

Noah's success didn't stop there. His victories and record-breaking runs made him a fan favorite and inspired young athletes around the world. Every race became a chance for him to set new goals and challenge himself to be better. Whether it was breaking records, winning medals, or simply running with passion, Noah proved that with determination and hard work, anything is possible.

THE JOURNEY TO THE OLYMPICS

For Noah Lyles, the Olympics represented the ultimate dream—an event where the world's best athletes come together to compete at the highest level. His journey to the Olympics was years in the making, filled with hard work, setbacks, and unforgettable moments. It wasn't just about running fast; it was about staying focused, overcoming challenges, and believing that one day, he would stand on the Olympic stage.

Noah's path to the Olympics began when he first started competing in major international competitions. His wins at the World Championships and other prestigious events put him on the radar of Olympic selectors, but the road to making the Olympic team was not easy. He had to prove himself in tough races, facing some of the world's fastest runners. The pressure was intense, but Noah knew that every race was a step closer to reaching his goal.

In 2020, Noah qualified for his first Olympic Games in Tokyo, Japan. His dream was about to come true. But getting there was only half the battle. The competition at the Olympics was fierce, with sprinters from all over the world, all hoping for gold. Noah faced incredible pressure, but he stayed calm and focused, knowing that he had prepared for this moment for years.

The journey to the Olympics taught Noah many lessons. He learned that patience was just as important as speed. He learned how to handle the nerves and pressure of competing on the biggest stage in the world. He also learned how to keep his passion for running alive, no matter how tough the road to the Olympics might be.

When Noah finally stepped onto the Olympic track, he knew it was the culmination of all his hard work and sacrifices. He didn't just run for himself; he ran for everyone who supported him along the way—his family, coaches, fans, and every young athlete who dreamed of following in his footsteps. His journey to the Olympics showed that with determination, belief in yourself, and a love for what you do, you can achieve your biggest dreams.

Noah Lyle's journey to the Olympics wasn't without its challenges. Leading up to the 2020 Tokyo Olympics, the world faced the global COVID-19 pandemic, which forced the postponement of the Games for an entire year. This was a tough moment for all athletes, but for Noah, it meant extra time to stay focused, train harder, and make sure he was in peak condition for the big moment. While many athletes struggled with the uncertainty, Noah used the extra time to perfect his technique and work on his mental strength.

Throughout the next year, Noah continued to shine in international competitions. He won medals and set new personal bests, keeping his momentum going and showing the world that he was more than ready for the Olympics. His confidence grew as he showed up at every event with an unstoppable mindset, making it clear that he was one of the fastest sprinters in the world.

When the Olympics finally arrived in 2021, Noah had already accomplished so much—but he knew this was his moment to go for gold. His Olympic journey wasn't just about his speed on the track, but also about his ability to stay calm under pressure. He didn't let the spotlight distract him; instead, he focused on doing his best, remembering all the hard work he had put in over the years.

At the Tokyo Olympics, Noah ran with everything he had, racing against the best sprinters in the world. Although he didn't bring home the gold, his experience at the Olympics taught him valuable lessons about the importance of resilience, perseverance, and handling tough competition. He knew that every race, win or lose, was another step toward his ultimate goals.

The Olympics were just one milestone in Noah's journey, but they were a reminder of how far he had come. It wasn't just about reaching the top—it was about the heart and determination he put into every race. For Noah, the journey to the Olympics showed that every challenge, setback, and victory played an important part in shaping the athlete he had become. The road to the Olympics was just the beginning of even bigger dreams ahead.

CHAPTER 5: INSPIRING THE WORLD

Noah Lyles' journey has inspired countless people around the world. From a young kid with big dreams to one of the fastest sprinters in the world, Noah's story is a testament to the power of perseverance, hard work, and self-belief. His rise to the top shows that no dream is too big and no goal is too far out of reach if you're willing to put in the effort.

Noah has always been vocal about how important it is to stay true to yourself and your dreams, no matter what obstacles come your way. Through his challenges and setbacks, he learned that it's not about avoiding failure but about how you bounce back from it. He's a role model for young athletes who face difficulties in their own lives, showing them that it's okay to fail, as long as you get up and keep moving forward.

His victories and incredible performances on the track have sparked hope and inspiration in others. When he breaks records or wins gold, it's not just a personal achievement—it's a moment that shows the world what's possible when you work hard and believe in yourself. Noah has proven that anyone can reach the top if they stay committed to their goals, no matter how challenging the road may be.

Off the track, Noah uses his platform to inspire kids to chase their dreams. He often speaks about the importance of never giving up, and encouraging others to stay positive and focused on their journeys. His story teaches that greatness doesn't happen by accident; it's something you build day by day with effort, determination, and a willingness to learn.

Noah's impact goes beyond track and field. He is a symbol of hope, showing that with hard work and the right mindset, you can overcome anything. His story is an inspiration to dream big, push through challenges, and always keep striving for your best—because the world is full of possibilities.

SHARING HIS STORY WITH OTHERS

Noah Lyles knows that his journey to becoming one of the world's fastest sprinters is about more than just winning races. He believes that his story can inspire others, especially young athletes, to pursue their dreams and never give up—no matter what challenges they face. That's why he takes every opportunity to share his experiences, struggles, and triumphs with others.

Noah Lyles

Whether it's speaking at schools, sharing his experiences on social media, or giving interviews, Noah makes it a point to encourage others to keep pushing forward. He talks about the hard work and dedication it took to get where he is, and he's open about the setbacks and injuries he faced along the way. By being honest about the struggles, he shows that success isn't just about winning—it's about learning from mistakes, growing stronger, and keeping a positive mindset.

Noah also uses his platform to teach kids that being a great athlete is about more than just physical talent. He often shares how important it is to believe in yourself, to stay focused, and to stay true to who you are. His message is clear: you don't have to be perfect to succeed; you just have to keep trying, learn from each experience, and never give up on your dreams.

Through his story, Noah encourages young athletes to take their own journeys seriously, to work hard in whatever sport they love, and to believe that they too can achieve great things. His story isn't just about sprinting—it's about resilience, heart, and the belief that anything is possible if you put your mind to it.

By sharing his story with others, Noah not only inspires the next generation of athletes but also leaves a lasting impact on anyone who hears it. He reminds us all that no matter where we start, with enough determination and hard work, we can reach heights we never imagined.

ADVICE FOR KIDS WITH BIG DREAMS

Noah Lyles knows what it's like to have big dreams and the determination to make them come true. His advice to kids who want to achieve their dreams, whether in sports or any other area, is simple yet powerful: stay focused, keep working hard, and believe in yourself.

1. Believe in Yourself
Noah always reminds kids that believing in yourself is the first step toward making any dream a reality. Even when things get tough or when others doubt you, always trust that you can succeed. Confidence is key. If you believe in your skills and your potential, it will help you push through challenges and keep moving forward.

2. Work Hard Every Day
Dreams don't come true without hard work. Noah's success on the track didn't happen by chance—it was the result of countless hours of training, practice, and sacrifice. Whether you want to be a great athlete, artist, or anything else, putting in the effort every single day is the most important part of reaching your goals.

Noah Lyles

3. Embrace Challenges and Setbacks
No one's journey is perfect, and setbacks are a natural part of life. Noah has faced his share of injuries and losses, but instead of giving up, he learned from each challenge. His advice is to see mistakes and challenges as learning opportunities. Each time you fall, get back up stronger and smarter.

4. Never Stop Learning
Noah emphasizes the importance of always being willing to learn, whether it's from a coach, a teammate, or even a mistake. Growth comes from being open to new ideas and constantly trying to improve. Stay curious, stay humble, and always look for ways to get better.

5. Stay Positive and Have Fun
Even with all the hard work, Noah reminds kids to have fun along the way. When you enjoy what you're doing, it's easier to stay motivated and keep going, even when things get tough. Keep a positive attitude, stay focused on the fun parts of chasing your dreams, and don't forget to enjoy the journey.

6. Set Goals and Keep Pushing
Noah encourages kids to set both short-term and long-term goals. Breaking big dreams down into smaller steps makes them feel more achievable. Whether it's

Noah Lyles

improving your skills, achieving a personal best, or working toward a bigger goal like a championship or a big performance, setting goals helps keep you on track and gives you something to strive for.

Noah's journey shows that with dedication, hard work, and a belief in yourself, anything is possible. His message to kids is clear: big dreams take time, effort, and patience, but if you stay focused and never give up, you can achieve amazing things!

CONCLUSION

Noah Lyles' journey from a young dreamer to one of the world's fastest sprinters is a powerful reminder of what's possible when you work hard, stay focused, and believe in yourself. His story isn't just about breaking records or winning medals—it's about the lessons he's learned along the way: the importance of resilience, perseverance, and the power of chasing your dreams, no matter how big they are.

Noah's success on the track is a result of years of dedication, training, and overcoming challenges. But what truly makes his story inspiring is his message to others: that anyone, no matter their background or the obstacles they face, can achieve greatness if they stay committed to their goals.

For kids with big dreams, Noah shows that success is not just about talent—it's about hard work, the belief in yourself, and the willingness to keep pushing forward, even when things get tough. His journey teaches us all that dreams are worth chasing, and with the right mindset, there's no limit to what you can accomplish.

As Noah continues to race toward new goals and inspire others, his story serves as a beacon for future athletes and dreamers everywhere. It's a reminder that no matter where you start, with dedication, fo
cus, and heart, anything is possible.

FUN FACTS ABOUT NOAH LYLES

1. He Loves Music: Noah Lyles is a big fan of music, especially hip-hop. He often listens to his favorite songs to pump himself up before races.

2. Young Start: Noah's track journey began at just **6 years old** when he joined his first track team. His early love for running grew into a passion that would define his life.

3. The Family Athlete: Both Noah and his brother, Josephus Lyles, are sprinters, and they've raced together in competitions. The Lyles brothers are a powerhouse duo in track and field.

4. A Creative Sprinter: Besides running, Noah is also creative and enjoys photography and filming videos. He

has shared some of his personal content, showing his fun side off the track.

5. Super Speedy in Practice: When Noah isn't racing, he's constantly working to be faster, and he loves doing **flying sprints**, where he accelerates into top speed to improve his form and speed.

6. His Nickname: Fans sometimes call him "the King of the 200 meters" because of his incredible dominance in the event, especially after winning gold at the 2019 World Championships.

7. He's a Showman: Before races, Noah is known for his energetic and charismatic personality, often pumping up the crowd with his fun antics and big smiles.

8. A Positive Attitude: Noah always tries to stay positive, even after losses. He believes every race is an opportunity to learn, grow, and come back stronger.

9. Olympic Inspiration: Noah looked up to legendary sprinters like Usain Bolt and always dreamed of racing on the Olympic stage. He now follows in their footsteps as one of the best sprinters in the world.

10. First Big Win: His very first international gold medal was won in 2016 at the World Junior Championships in

the 200 meters. He was just 19 years old and showed the world he was ready for bigger things.

11. His Fastest Race Ever: Noah's personal best in the 200 meters is a 19.50-second run, making him the third-fastest man in history in the event—right behind the legendary Usain Bolt!

12. Has a Sweet Tooth: Despite being an elite athlete, Noah has a soft spot for chocolate, and he's not afraid to enjoy a treat every now and then!

NOAH LYLES TRIVIA QUIZ

1. What is Noah Lyles' personal best in the 200 meters?
   a) 19.90 seconds
   b) 19.50 seconds
   c) 19.70 seconds
   d) 20.10 seconds

2. Where was Noah Lyles born?
   a) Miami, Florida
   b) Gainesville, Florida
   c) Atlanta, Georgia
   d) Los Angeles, California

3. What medal did Noah Lyles win in the 200 meters at the 2019 World Championships?
   a) Bronze
   b) Silver
   c) Gold
   d) No medal

4. Which event does Noah Lyles primarily compete in?
   a) 100 meters
   b) 200 meters
   c) 400 meters
   d) 800 meters

5. Noah Lyles made his Olympic debut in which year?
   a) 2016
   b) 2020 (held in 2021)
   c) 2012
   d) 2024

6. What is Noah Lyles' brother's name, who is also a sprinter?
   a) Josephus Lyles
   b) Jonathan Lyles
   c) Jared Lyles
   d) Jason Lyles

7. What is Noah Lyles' favorite way to get pumped up before races?

Noah Lyles

a) Listening to music
b) Watching motivational videos
c) Doing yoga
d) Playing video games

8. In which event did Noah Lyles win his first international gold medal?
a) 100 meters
b) 200 meters at the World Junior Championships
c) 4x100 meters relay
d) 400 meters at the World Championships

9. Which sprinter did Noah Lyles admire growing up and still looks up to today?
a) Carl Lewis
b) Usain Bolt
c) Michael Johnson
d) Justin Gatlin

10. Noah Lyles is known for his energy and showmanship before races. What is his nickname?
a) King of Speed
b) The Fastest Sprinter
c) King of the 200 meters
d) Lightning Lyles

ANSWERS:

Noah Lyles

1. b) 19.50 seconds
2. b) Gainesville, Florida
3. c) Gold
4. b) 200 meters
5. b) 2020 (held in 2021)
6. a) Josephus Lyles
7. a) Listening to music
8. b) 200 meters at the World Junior Championships
9. b) Usain Bolt
10. c) King of the 200 meters

Made in the USA
Las Vegas, NV
15 January 2025